IMAGES
of America

BLACK HILLS NATIONAL FOREST
HARNEY PEAK AND THE
HISTORIC FIRE LOOKOUT TOWERS

D1710225

The historic Black Hills National Forest entrance sign welcomes visitors to the area.

ON THE COVER: Visitors enjoy the view from the Harney Peak Lookout Tower. Located in the center of the granite core of the Black Hills, Harney Peak offers some of the most spectacular scenery in the United States. Today, 1.4 billion years of geologic history are exposed to view.

IMAGES
of America

BLACK HILLS NATIONAL FOREST
HARNEY PEAK AND THE
HISTORIC FIRE LOOKOUT TOWERS

Jan Cerney and Roberta Sago

ARCADIA
PUBLISHING

Published by Arcadia Publishing
Charleston, South Carolina

Printed in the United States of America

Library of Congress Control Number: 2010931932

For all general information, please contact Arcadia Publishing:
Telephone 843-853-2070
Fax 843-853-0044
E-mail sales@arcadiapublishing.com
For customer service and orders:
Toll-Free 1-888-313-2665

Visit us on the Internet at www.arcadiapublishing.com

CONTENTS

ACKNOWLEDGMENTS

We would like to thank the Black Hills National Forest and Frank Carroll, the planning and public relations officer, for their support of this publication. We are grateful for the assistance of many other Forest Service members, including Michael Hilton and Michael Engelhart, both of Custer, South Dakota, and the staff at the Bearlodge Ranger District Office in Sundance, Wyoming. Many others helped us by providing photographs and information. They include the following people and organizations: Karen Wattenmaker; Terre Houska; Rocky Courchaine and the Crook County Museum in Sundance, Wyoming; June Johnson; Dixie Boyle; Ginger Olson; and Peggy Sanders. Inspiration for this project came from the Black Hills National Forest Historical Collection at the Leland D. Case Library for Western Historical Studies at Black Hills State University. Many of the photographs and much of our research came from this collection. Photographs without credit lines in the description are from this collection.

INTRODUCTION

Fire. It is a most elemental force of nature that has shaped our history and the landscape. Man's relationship with fire is complex; it can be both friend and foe. As a tool, it can provide warmth and a means of preparing meals that sustain us. But it can also be an instrument of great destruction—a threat to life and natural resources. And yet, for millions of years Mother Nature routinely used fire to "clean house." The life cycle of many varieties of plants depends on fire. Low-intensity fires are an important part of maintaining balanced ecosystems.

At one time, the bounty of our natural resources seemed endless. Commercial interests indiscriminately harvested our forest with selfish and wasteful abandon. Gifford Pinchot, the first chief of the Forest Service, observed that in the Gay Nineties wastefulness of timber was considered a virtue not a crime. In the mid-19th century, people began to understand that the forests could be depleted and that deforestation had other serious consequences. The conservation movement began to develop.

One early advocate for forest conservation was Franklin B. Hough (pronounced Huff). Due to his efforts and those of like-minded people, the Division of Forestry was created within the US Department of Agriculture on June 30, 1886. Hough became the first superintendent of this new division. The efforts of early conservation advocates were further rewarded when the Forest Reserves Act of 1891 was passed. President Harrison created the first reserve, the Yellowstone Timber Reserve, on March 30, 1891. However, there were no procedures for administering the reserves until the passage of Civil Service Act of June 4, 1897. By 1901, Gifford Pinchot began introducing management procedures for the Forest Reserves. The Department of Agriculture's Bureau of Forestry and the Forestry division of the Department of the interior were responsible for overseeing the Forest Reserves. In 1905, these two entities were combined to create the US Forest Service. The Forest Reserves were renamed National Forests in 1907.

On February 22, Pres. Grover Cleveland signed a proclamation creating the Black Hills Forest Reserve. An area approximately 120 miles long and 40 miles wide was included in this reserve. Seth Bullock, a prominent pioneer and businessman from Deadwood, South Dakota, served as the second forest supervisor of the Black Hills Forest Reserve. He was a supporter of the conservation cause and had been involved in the creation of the Yellowstone Forest Reserve. While local industries chaffed at governmental protection of the forestlands, he understood the same industries dependent on forest products in the long term needed responsible management of those resources. During his tenure, the Black Hills Forest Reserve served as a laboratory for testing many of Pinchot's ideas. In March of 1897, a delegation, including the General Council of the Homestake Mining Co. of Lead, South Dakota, visited Pres. William McKinley to request that the Black Hills be removed from the Forest Reserves. Due to this pressure, the Civil Service Act of was amended. This was the beginning of the concept of multiple use of forestland.

In addition to irresponsible logging practices, fire was determined to be a serious threat to the timber supply. Early fire detection consisted of lookouts patrolling particular areas on horseback.

This was ineffective for observing the vast area that needed to be protected. Lookouts were then stationed on several peaks throughout the forest. For the first couple of years, tents were the only accommodations provided. In 1911, the first lookout structure was built on Custer Peak. A cabin was constructed on Cement Ridge the following year.

The first structures were wooden. In the 1930s and 1940s, many were replaced with more durable stone structures built by the Civilian Conservation Corps (CCC). The CCC was also trained to fight forest fires. Then, in the 1940s, steel structures started replacing the wood towers.

As technology has changed, lookout towers have become less of a linchpin in fire detection and many were removed. There are still about five lookouts that are staffed during the summer months, and they are popular destinations for hikers, bikers, and even folks out for a Sunday drive. Some are accessible by roads, while some are more remote and only accessible by the most stalwart hiker.

In her 2006 paper, Nancy Remington identifies 25 lookout towers that have existed throughout the Black Hills. We have found photographs of each of these and have actually visited some. Now we will take you on a tour of the Black Hills Fire Lookout Towers. They make up an important and interesting facet of this nation's history. As we travel through time and introduce some of the many men and women who have served as fire lookouts, we hope you will enjoy the trip.

One

EARLY FIRE DETECTION

The primary purpose of fire lookout personnel is to provide early detection of forest fires. Forest Service lookout employees, or volunteers, are also trained to coordinate communications and dispatch people, equipment, and materials to fires. They are responsible for keeping fire crews informed as to the nature of the fire and weather conditions. The trusty tools of the trade are lookouts' knowledge of the area, a fire finder, a map, binoculars, and a communication system.

This smoke was viewed from Harney Peak. By this point, the lookout on duty had used the Osborne Fire Finder to locate the fire and called another fire lookout tower nearby, if available, to triangulate the location. After this was done, the lookout on duty determined the location and called it in to the dispatch center. To the lookout, white smoke signifies a grass fire, and dark smoke is from pitch or heavier fuel. A rookie lookout's greatest fear is missing a fire and having someone else "pick up a fire" for him.

In the early 1930s, W.B. Osborne, a member of the Forest Service, designed the Osborne Fire Finder. The Fire Finder is an alidade used to find a directional bearing. It rotates 360 degrees and is accurate and requires no special operative power.

To use the Osborne Fire Finder, the lookout must line up the hair in the front sight. When the hair is aligned with the smoke, a horizontal reading in degrees and minutes is taken. A vertical angle reading is additionally recorded by using the measurement on the sliding metal piece on the rear sight. The miles are then estimated between the tower and the smoke sighted using the metal tape on the Fire Finder. The lookout uses a pull-down map to pinpoint the area of the fire. Often the lookout communicates with another nearby lookout tower to coordinate the line of sight, resulting in better accuracy. In this image, the lookout is taking a vertical reading.

The tape for delineating line of sight and estimating distance of a fire from the lookout point is clearly visible on this Osborne Fire Finder. Before closing the station for the night, lookouts were sometimes required to clean the Fire Finder, release tension on cross wires and distance tape, and remove the map and store in a dry place. Lookouts were advised not to use the Fire Finder as a table for cups, ashtrays, binoculars, clothing, or books, but to keep it clean and orderly.

The map used to locate the smoke is clearly visible. The lookout lines up the column of smoke with the front and rear sight of the Fire Finder. The lookout then looks under the metal tape connected to the sights and finds the center of the fire. The fire can then be tracked on the wall map to plot the range, section, and township. Each circle on the map represents a fire tower and its area.

As soon as smoke was located, it was called in to a dispatcher. In front of the dispatcher is the map board. Visible are the magnets in the center of each circle that secure the strings to be drawn across the board to pinpoint where the reported bearings intersect. Ground crews were then dispatched to the location of the smoke.

Pictured is a telephone used at Bear Mountain. The early lookout towers used telephones to communicate between other towers and the dispatch center. The CCC members and other workers peeled poles and strung telephone lines throughout the Black Hills.

In 1936, trainees inspect telephone lines, which were susceptible to inclement weather conditions. Downed lines interrupted the communication system. Forest supervisor Clarence C. Averill took this photograph. As supervisor from 1948 to 1953, he pioneered the use of communications between ranger stations. (C.C. Averill.)

A type SV radiophone, dated 1940, is being used in this image, allowing for two-way communication. Early radios required batteries until electricity was installed at the fire towers. Many types of radios replaced telephones as the communication system used in the lookout towers.

These unidentified forest supervisors met at Harney Peak in October 1925. The supervisors of the Black Hills National Forest through 1925 were H.G. Hamaker, 1897–1901; Seth Bullock, 1901–1906; John Fremont Smith, 1906–1907; Edwin M. Hamilton, 1908–1909; Paul D. Kelleter, 1909–1918; and George A. Duthie, 1918–1930. In 1910, the Black Hills National Forest was divided to create the Harney National Forest; they were remerged in 1954. The Harney National Forest Supervisors through 1925 were Richard P. Imes, 1910–1916; J.F. Connor, 1916–-1917; George Duthie, 1917–1918; and J.F. Connor, 1918–1935.

Known as the guardians of the Black Hills National Forest, these forest officers met at Merritt Ranger Station in 1926. Pictured from left to right are Rube Riley, Frank Blankenship, William Fay, Marion J. Webber, William Robinson, George Duthie, T.R. Cochran, ? Stahl, Manford Hickel, Leslie Graham, and F.J. Poch. By 1930, there were five fire lookout stations located on the high peaks of Custer Peak, Cement Ridge, Harney Peak, Bear Mountain, and Mount Coolidge. Mount Coolidge was maintained cooperatively by the State of South Dakota and the federal government.

Two

Harney Peak
Fire Lookout

Located four miles southwest of Mount Rushmore, Harney Peak, at an elevation of 7,242 feet, rises in the center of the granite core of the Black Hills. The Lakota Sioux call it Han Kaga, which means in Lakota the "center of the world." Surrounded by the spectacular needle formations and ponderosa pines, many visitors are awed by its beauty.

Forrester Max Jacobs of the Dominion Service, Canberra, Australia, took this photograph of Harney Peak on April 5, 1938. He is quoted as saying, "One of the most magnificent views I've seen in all my travels." Looking east, Harney Peak is the high point in the left center. General Harney observed the peak in 1855, and Lt. G.K. Warren named Harney Peak for Gen. William Selby Harney while on a survey expedition in 1857.

Wildlife frequently visits the peak. Mountain goats often are viewed within sight of the lookout tower; deer and elk can often be seen, too. Mountain goats were first introduced to the Black Hills in the 1920s. Some are descendants from those captured in Glacier National Park in Montana. A member of the antelope family, the white and black horned animals can be seen scaling the granite cliffs and high peaks. Their specially padded hooves offer traction that keeps them from slipping.

General Custer and his men attempted to climb the peak in 1874 but were hindered by darkness. Valentine T. McGillycuddy (pictured), a member of the Jenny expedition in 1875, was the first white man recorded to climb Harney Peak, but this was not his only mark of distinction. Born on Valentine's Day 1849, McGillycuddy graduated from Detroit Medical School at the age of 20. After practicing medicine and teaching at a medical college, he was lured to the West and joined several expeditions. In 1875, McGillycuddy came to Dakota Territory with the Jenney-Newton expedition as contract surgeon and topographer. It was then that the 26-year-old doctor used a fallen tree as a ladder to climb the steep granite of Harney Peak. (Minnilusa Historical Association.)

McGillycuddy served as field surgeon for General Crook and in 1876 became assistant post surgeon at Camp Robinson, where he met Crazy Horse. He became his friend, doctored his wife with tuberculosis, and tended to the dying Crazy Horse at Fort Robinson. McGillycuddy served as Indian agent at Pine Ridge from 1866 to 1879. He and his wife, Fanny, moved to Rapid City in 1888 when he was elected to the state constitutional convention in 1890 and was appointed South Dakota's surgeon general. McGillycuddy helped care for the injured during the Wounded Knee Massacre. He served as dean of the School of Mines from 1893 to 1897 and also became mayor of Rapid City in 1897. Over a decade later, he treated victims of influenza throughout the West.

The *Rapid City Daily Journal* on October 17, 1940, reported Valentine McGillycuddy's death as June 6, 1939, in Berkeley, California, at the age of 90, stating that his ashes were brought to Rapid City. Through cooperative efforts of the US Forest Service, a crypt was built in a new stone stairway leading to the top of Harney Peak, which would contain the urn holding his ashes. Lone Eagle regarded McGillycuddy as a great man and friend of the Sioux Nation. Engraved on the brass box containing the ashes was the inscription *"wasicu wakan."* When translated, it means "holy white man." The crypt is seen below the tower. (Jay Higgins.)

Present at the ceremony were an American Legion color guard; Forest Service officials; a nephew, Trant McGillycuddy, of Rapid City; and a grand-nephew, Michael McGillycuddy McNary of Arizona, formerly of Rapid City, who was attending the School of Mines at the time. E.A. Snow, supervisor of the Harney National Forest, led the group of about 15 men to the top of Harney Peak. Included in the legion color guard were fire chief George Engler, Art Jensen, Emil Wulf, and M.W. Seese. In addition to the two McGillycuddys and Lone Eagle, who paid homage to the former agent in the Sioux language, were Hugh Hamill, curator of the Sioux Indian museum in Rapid City; Carl Behrens; Forest Service and CCC officials; and M.E. Nystrom, of Custer, who made the crypt and built the new stone stairway. There were also about 20 CCC men at work near the peak. Some of his other friends accompanied the entourage to the base of the peak.

The Lakota holy man Nicholas Black Elk appeared on the top of Harney Peak in his great vision at the age of nine. It was during a serious illness that he received the vision and saw himself "standing on the highest mountain of them all, and round about beneath me was the whole hoop of the world." The Sacred Hoop has been explained as nature's most perfect form, a sacred symbol of life, the peoples' connection to the earth, and a web of relationship and respect with all things of the earth. During this vision, Black Elk was given the power to restore his people, who were suffering from white encroachment, the loss of their lands, and the loss of their sustenance, the buffalo.

When Black Elk was an old man, he told his story through his son Ben Black Elk (pictured), acting as interpreter, to poet John G. Neihardt. The resulting narrative shared about Lakota spirituality became the book *Black Elk Speaks*. Ben Black Elk appeared at Mount Rushmore for many years after World War II. He told many stories and posed for pictures with visitors. Ben was dubbed "fifth face on the mountain" and was photographed as often as 5,000 times a day.

Black Elk expressed his wish to stand on Harney Peak to Neihardt. In May 1931, Ben Black Elk, his father Black Elk, John Neihardt, and Neihardt's daughters Enid and Hilda made the trip. At the summit of Harney Peak, Black Elk appealed to the Great Spirit to let his people live. From his uplifted face, he shed tears of remorse, feeling that he done nothing to save his nation's hoop from becoming broken and scattered. Earlier he had remarked to his son Ben that if the thunder beings of the West should hear his voice, there should be a little thunder and a little rain. In spite of one of the worst droughts, the clouds gathered, thunder rumbled, and rain fell; and then just as quickly, the sky cleared.

In July 1911, President Taft split the Black Hills Forest Reserve into the Black Hills National Forest in the northern half of the hills and Harney National Forest in the southern half. Just four days later, Rufus J. Pilcher established the first lookout on Harney Peak, which consisted of a wooden crate with an alidade set on top, a Forest Service compass, and a pair of 5.5-power binoculars. Eventually, a table with legs set in cement replaced the wooden box. Pilcher and his brother carried their equipment to the peak by horseback. The next morning, he spotted the first fire from that lookout.

H.H. Hewitt was the first lookout assigned to Harney Peak and remained in charge until 1917, when Earl Emmons took over the job. In May 1919, a 12-foot-by-12-foot cabin was built just below the peak. Earl H. Emmons and his new bride went to the peak to live, thus giving her the distinction of being the first white woman to live on Harney Peak.

In 1920, the first lookout building was constructed on Harney Peak. Dynamite leveled the rock, and a 12-square-foot building with three windows on each side was erected. A flagpole was placed next to the building that would serve as a lookout for 18 years. The April 1909 edition of the *Custer County Chronicle* expressed concerns for fire patrol: "The Forest service men in the Black Hills are agitating for the establishment of stations for fire patrol upon Harney Peak and Terry Peak. It is a good scheme, and we hope the Government will take cognizance of the importance of such stations and the advantage that may accrue there from."

In 1921, the building was enlarged to 16 square feet, adding two more windows on each side. In 1922, Faye Beard became the first, and only, woman lookout at that time. Her husband, Paul J. Beard, was appointed forest guard in 1923, and Harry Edwards followed him in 1924. Edwards stayed on the peak two seasons, and in 1927 Ed Doberidge became the lookout. In 1928, William Fay served as lookout, followed in 1929 and 1930 by Doberidge. P.J. Hibbard then came on duty for 1931 and 1932, followed in 1933 by Glen M. Coe and in 1934 by John Endicott. Two CCC enrollees were detailed for lookout duty in 1935.

Howard Culver served as lookout on Harney in 1936 and 1937. The wooden building was torn down in 1938 to make way for a new lookout constructed of native stone. Howard, pictured on the left, became the first lookout in the newly constructed stone tower.

This Forest Service employee is using binoculars to scan the magnificent view from Harney Peak for signs of smoke. In April 1909, the *Custer County Chronicle* reported, "A lookout on each peak provided with a good field glass can view the entire Hill's territory and, with a phone line from each peak to the nearest established phone line, in case of fire they could save much valuable time in mobilizing to save property. The *Chronicle* deems this an imperative need and is willing to favor the project and urge its early fulfillment."

Members of the Forest Service stand in front of the Harney Peak Lookout in 1938. Forest Service supervisors at that time were Theodore Krueger and E.A. Snow. Snow resisted the pressure to overharvest the forests for the war effort and helped design shelterbelts throughout the Great Plains. Krueger utilized the CCC labor from 27 camps to implement intensive forestry practices.

A supervisor's meeting was held on Harney Peak in 1925 to deal with a fire problem. Those present are, from left to right, Hatton, Harry Peck, Thompson, Hamel, Douglas, and an unidentified man.

Members of the CCC stand on the steps of Harney Peak Lookout. Franklin D. Roosevelt issued an executive order on April 5, 1933, creating the agency of Emergency Conservation Work, which later became known as the Civilian Conservation Corps (CCC). During the mid-1930s, many CCC camps were established in the Black Hills. The purpose of the CCC was to provide employment and vocational training for youthful citizens of the United States, as well as for war veterans. Camp Doran, located five miles east of Custer, provided the labor force for the construction of a new tower at Harney Peak.

CCC workers are seen beginning construction of the new lookout tower on Harney Peak. The old lookout building was torn down in April 1938, and construction on the stone tower began. The CCC made a tremendous lasting contribution to the Black Hills with its many forest improvements and recreation projects.

In addition to construction projects, the CCC spent thousands of days on thinning the forest, fire prevention, and suppression. They removed debris, constructed firebreaks, and built and staffed lookouts. The CCC constructed 1,400 miles of telephone lines, over 1,528 miles of truck and fire trails, and devoted more than 77,000 man-days of firefighting.

189. On the Trail to Harney Peak aboard a Burro, Black Hills, S. D. "See America First."

A 1938 *South Dakota Guide* described the trail to Harney Peak. Nearby were stables where burros could be procured for the climb up Harney Peak. A beautiful, winding footpath led through the woods to the peak. About halfway up was a wayside spring, and from this point the trail became steeper and arrived at a ladder, which hikers climbed to reach the lookout station. From this vantage point, the granite backside of Mount Rushmore, which was in the process of being carved, could be seen to the east. Mount Coolidge with its tower rose to the south. Terry and Custer Peak could be viewed in the north. A person assuming the position as fireguard sat in a glass-walled fire station and used a swivel telescope swinging over a map to locate the first sign of smoke. He communicated with rangers throughout the Black Hills with a telephone. About 10,000 people climbed the summit annually, and many asked, "Don't you get awfully lonesome up here, all by yourself?"

In the 1930s, the burros that transported tourists to the top of Harney Peak were let loose when the trail rides were discontinued. Today, descendants of those early burros wander at will and entertain the tourists almost to the point of being a nuisance by blocking roadways in Custer State Park. These burros are known as "begging burros" or "brazen burros," as they poke their noses in car windows begging for food. Current policy, however, prohibits feeding park wildlife. In order to maintain their population, several are auctioned off every year during the annual bison auction.

Burro Beggars

Tourist businesses made photographs of burros in the Black Hills into postcards. The summary on the back of one of the postcards reads, "Be on the look out for mountain burros as you drive the Iron Mount Road between Mount Rushmore and the State Game Lodge. These amiable little fellows are always looking for a hand out."

Located on the highest point in South Dakota, which is also the highest point east of the Rockies, Harney Peak Lookout was built over a two-year period from 1939 to 1940 and is listed on the National Historic Lookout Register. CCC recruits were assigned to two or three weeks of conditioning before they began work on projects. This physical-hardening process was necessary in order to handle the strenuous projects assigned to them.

Reinforced concrete was used on the bottom-level floors. The 30-inch outer walls were lined with hollow tiles. Many of the young recruits had no prior construction skills and learned with proper leadership from experienced men. CCC recruits also learned about forest culture, forest protection, erosion control, flood control, irrigation and drainage, transportation improvements, structural improvements, range development, wildlife, and landscape and recreation projects.

A woman identified as Mrs. Howard Culver in the photograph above uses a trowel to lay stone. Construction of the tower began in April 1938, and by November 3 of that year 7,000 surface stones, 500 bricks, and 15,000 hollow tiles had been used.

Men are mixing cement and framing in a window in these two images. From April 1938 to November of the same year, 200 tons of sand, 32,800 pounds of cement, 500 pieces of reinforced steel and angle iron, 300 poles averaging 25 feet in length, 20 kegs of nails, 1,000 feet of steel cable, and 1,300 pounds of steel wire had been used.

French Creek provided the rock for the outer walls and walkways. Horse-drawn sleds transported the rock in winter when there was snow on the ground, but when the snow disappeared a horse-drawn, two-wheeled cart was used. The cart was capable of carrying from 15 to 20 stones and the driver to the base of the peak.

Pack Trains hauled many supplies up the side of the mountain to build the Harney Peak Tower. Among the building materials transported in this manner were a total of 1,328 sacks of cement and two carloads of sand, which were brought up the steep slopes to the cable system.

From the base, cables were used to pull the cart up the steep incline. Neil Hamilton, the project supervisor, estimated that approximately 7,500 face rocks were needed for the tower. The rock was handpicked and transported by truck to a stockpile at the foot of the trail.

A gin pole is an upright mast, guyed at the top to maintain vertical position, and is equipped with hoisting equipment. A gin pole is used for tower work and functions as a safety device for lifting when used properly. The gin pole consists of a pulley assembly to provide mechanical advantage when lifting, a pole to gain height for the lift, and a clamp assembly to attach everything to the tower.

Foreman Leo Harbach of CCC Camp F-23 supervises work at Harney Peak. A pulley system was used to move building materials up the steep slope of Harney Peak. Later, Harbach would become the fire chief of the Custer Volunteer Fire Department and would serve for many years. Because of his dedicated service, the fire department building and a park were named in his honor. Harbach was also noted for developing a type of crew lights that could be used when fighting night fires—he was constantly training and upgrading firefighting methods.

The roof went on during the 19th week of work. Sheet copper tops the tower roof and was grounded from lightning by 3.5-inch copper cables. Carpenter Bill Harris carefully maneuvers his way around the top of the tower.

Two men complete the roof so the copper can be added at the final stage; adding copper reduced the danger of lightning strikes. Carpenter Bill Harris is on the left in this photograph.

Mrs. Howard Culver stands on the roof of the Harney Peak Lookout, the highest point east of the Rockies.

Many people were involved in the construction of the tower at Harney Peak. Some of those involved in the administrative and construction phase were A.E. Snow, supervisor of the Harney National Forest; Neil Hamilton, project supervisor; masons M.E. Nystrom and his son Scott; Elmer Cummings, excavator; William Harris, carpenter; Leo Harbach, transportation; Lt. L.F. Erickson, commander of Camp Doran; and, indeed, all the CCC workers who provided the physical manpower.

The rough work was completed in 1938, and the finishing touches were applied in 1939. The new tower was complete with electricity and running water pumped from a reservoir, built in 1935, located just below the tower.

Howard Culver was the first to man the tower, and in 1965 Homer Baker became the last USDA Forest Service employee at the Harney Peak Tower. At that time, it was turned over to the Department of Game, Fish, and Parks. They manned the tower for two years, and then it was returned to the Forest Service who then boarded it up in 1967. The architecturally significant tower was placed on the National Register in 1982.

As a warning to airplanes, the US War Department erected the blinker light on the summit of Harney Peak.

CCC workers built the stone and wood concession building near Harney Peak in 1941–1942. Knotty pine finished off the ceiling, a fireplace was included in the interior, and a space for a lunchroom, kitchen, and a bedroom was also planned. The projected cost was estimated at $2,500. A stone latrine was also in the plans to accompany the concession building. The estimated material cost was estimated at $500 for this facility. (J. Roeser Jr.)

In 1891, a group of businessmen from Custer, South Dakota, proposed the creation of a lake to add to the recreational and scenic attractions of the vicinity. They selected a site seven miles from town surrounded by rocky outcroppings. To the dismay of many of the first visitors, early accommodations were rustic. Options included camping and then a rough log hotel. In 1896, the Sylvan Lake Hotel was built, nestled in the granite needle formations that overlooked the man-made lake. The 66-room, three-story structure was lavishly trimmed in gingerbread filigree. Unfortunately this hotel was destroyed by fire, and a new hotel was built in 1936–1937.

The needle formations, composed of the Black Hills granite core, have eroded for countless centuries. Wind and weather have whittled magnificent shapes of splendor that jut out of the pine forests in imaginative chiseled forms. The northern 14 miles of South Dakota Highway 87, also known as the Needles Highway, wends through these granite spires. Construction of this road in 1919 required 150,000 pounds of dynamite. Part of the Peter Norbeck Scenic Byway, this road provides a picturesque drive.

Granite spires of the needle formations appear in the background, as supervisor Marion J. Webber and Dana Parkinson of the Washington Office are photographed by Fred R. Johnson on the Harney Trail in May 1945. Webber served as supervisor from 1944 to 1954, during which time he mobilized forest resources for the war effort, fought his own war against the pine beetle, and organized the western plains grasslands.

M.E. Nystrom's cut-down Model A Ford was the first vehicle to make it to the top of Harney Peak. The unusual vehicle was about 30 inches in width with a four-speed transmission. Hap McCarty operated the concession on the peak in the 1950s. He purchased the Model A Ford to haul supplies back and forth.

In 1952, Hap McCarty bought a jeep in order to take friends to Harney Peak. The requests became so numerous that he began jeep rides to the peak as a business. Don and Betty Clifford, operators of Sylvan Lake Resort, operated the business in 1957. Land management action closed the Harney Peak jeep rides in 1968 because of soil erosion.

Riding the trail to Harney Peak is one way to reach the summit. The north trail to the peak is the most popular horseback trail, although there are 50 miles of Harney Range trails and 14 trailheads, with 12 to choose from for hiking.

In 1966, plans were in place for a Harney Peak development intended to make this area the recreational center of the Black Hills. By this time, 14,000 persons a year visited Harney Peak by either hiring jeep rides, riding horseback, or by hiking to the summit and the tower. The hardy visitors who have made it to the tower have described the view from the summit as magnificent and the tower as castle-like in appearance, or perhaps even resembling a fortress. Luckily, the unique Harney Peak Tower and its pristine scenery will be preserved for posterity.

The Forest Service felt there was a need to accommodate the increasing number of visitors. The development plan included a proposed tramway, a visitor center, a convenience food and beverage service outlet, and an Indian cultural center at the summit. The proposed plan speculated that the increased visitor total would rise to 500,000 visitors a year and would keep tourists in the Black Hills longer. The total cost of the project was projected at $2,194,000 by the year 1970.

However, the proposed plan alarmed the general public, who formed the Committee for Preservation of Harney Peak. Many town meetings were held all over the Black Hills, rejecting the development for fear that it would ruin the pristine scenery. The public outcry and other logistic reasons in regard to public safety atop the peak; the impact of 500,000 persons on a wilderness area; the unsuitability of a tramline for esthetic, cultural, and historic reasons; as well as other concerns prevented the development from being implemented.

Sen. George McGovern proposed a bill to Congress that established the Black Elk Wilderness in 1980. Named in honor of the holy man Black Elk and his vision, this wilderness area encompassed 10,700 acres surrounding and including Harney Peak. The proposed bill stated, "In short, it is not only important to preserve the area surrounding Harney Peak for generations to come so that they might enjoy a taste of wilderness, but it is historically, morally, and spiritually so very right that we do so."

Over a period of years, the tower began to deteriorate with rotting wood, broken windows, and loose stones. The consensus of the general public was to restore it rather than tear it down. The Forest Service received congressional funding, and in 1996 Hillside Construction was awarded the tower contract. In turn, Hillside Construction asked Dakota Badlands Outfitters to move between eight and nine tons of lumber and other supplies to the top of Harney Peak by pack mules, considering motorized vehicles were not allowed. Being experienced in the art of trail rides, the employees of Dakota Badlands Outfitters used mules named Jenny, Judy, and Festus, and 30 other head of horses and other mules to accomplish the job the old fashioned way, much as it was done in 1938–1939.

Three

CUSTER PEAK AND NORTHERN BLACK HILLS FIRE LOOKOUT TOWERS

Custer Peak is easily identified by its distinctive cone shape. The peak was named for Gen. George A. Custer, who stopped close to this peak while leading an exploration party through the Black Hills in 1874. The first lookout building and telephone line were constructed on Custer Peak in 1911. Manford Hickel helped build the first lookout on the peak. Soon to turn 19 years old, Hickel applied for work at the Forest Service Office on May 31, 1911.

Forest ranger Manford Hickel is pictured in this image entitled, "Ranger Meeting on a Stump."
From left to right are M.J. Webber, Manford Hickel, F.J. Poch, ? Gill, and Charles Webber. Before
Hickel became a forest ranger, William Wiehe, the assistant supervisor of the Black Hills National
Forest, hired him to help build a lookout on Custer Peak. Hickel was paid $2 for each eight-hour
day, six days a week; for all work over eight hours a day, he would get 25¢ per hour. Forest assistant
Homer Reed and another man, William McGee, assisted him. A livery team and driver were
hired to take the men on an all-day trip to Custer Peak.

Continuing with the Hickel story, the liveryman left with the team and wagon the next morning, and the men scaled Custer Peak, where they tried to level off a spot on solid rock on which the cabin would be built. On the following day, they swamped out a wagon road on the west side, so a team could get through with a small load of lumber. On June 4, Homer Reed walked to the Jusco ranch to arrange for them to haul lumber from Dumont siding to Custer Peak. The next day, Jusco delivered three loads of lumber—one trip per day—to the base of the peak. The following week, Jusco made a green aspen sled and skidded the loads the last 400 meters to the top. Hickel started working on the old Merritt Ranger District in 1911. The Merritt District and the Boxelder District were later consolidated with the Nemo District, and through the period of 1925–1936 Hickel served as district ranger for the Nemo District. Manford Hickel is pictured here with Ranger Irvin V. Case in September 12, 1975.

Ranger Frank Smith joined the crew, and he and Homer Reed located and staked out the route for the telephone line, while McGee and Hickel worked on the 12-foot-by-12-foot lookout building, with a 4-foot open porch built around the outside. After the building's completion, they began work on cutting and peeling 115 telephone poles and 114 pitch stubs, clearing the telephone line right-of-way, digging and setting all the posts, and then wiring the poles to stubs. They were hired to build 3.5 miles of telephone line from Custer Peak to Bull Dog Ranch. By September 8, all the work had been completed. Frank Tower assumed the job as the first lookout before the men left. Frank Tower (left) and Rochford ranger Lionel Anderson are seen below looking for trouble on the grounded telephone lines near the Custer Peak Lookout.

The building with the cupola, pictured in 1939, replaced the original lookout sometime in the 1930s. Consulting architect W. Ellis Groben began his description of a suggested design for another new tower with the following words: "Because of its elevated position, a very dominating one, and its visibility from the main highway through this locality, the Custer Peak Lookout Tower attracts unusual public attention. Its commanding and expansive view of the surrounding countryside as well as the relative ease with which it may be reached by motor makes it an exceptionally attractive observation point. In view of these facts and the possibility of replacing the present structure by a new one in the near future, the accompanying tentative sketch has been prepared as a suggestion indicative of the possibilities of this particular site."

19783

Groben continued, "The existing wooden lookout tower while, perhaps, sufficient to serve all the practical purposes for which it was intended, is not a very appropriate structure to occupy such a strategic and conspicuous site in the Black Hills." Groben's recommendations specified that the new lookout be "expressive of its particular environment." Using local stone and a primitive, rugged, and massive architectural style would "contribute to the creation of a bold and picturesque watchtower."

Further recommendations suggested that the various rooms to be few, and the accommodations confined to only those absolutely necessary. Providing toilet facilities for both sexes was also suggested. Recommendations were made to extend the approach road to the site, facilitating use by the general public "to whom it will become a most unique point of interest in this highly travelled region, where its advertising potentialities alone, on behalf of effective Forest Service fire protective measures, are not to be disregarded." (Roberta Sago.)

Designed by architect W. Ellis Groben and built in 1941, the stone tower is listed on National Historical Lookout Register. The stone lookout, which blends into the environment as designed, reaches an elevation of 6,804 feet and is located seven miles south of Lead and nine miles south of Deadwood. An outside stairway leads to a glass-enclosed crow's nest. The US Forest Service operates the Custer Peak Lookout.

Pictured is a section of land damaged by the McVey fire. Note that many trees were broken off several feet from the ground by cyclonic winds that occurred during the run of the fire. Approximately 1,755 men fought the intensely burning blaze. After the fire, the area experienced three years of heavy flooding. As a result of this fire, a law was passed regulating open fires and providing penalties for the violation.

Taken approximately at 1:00 p.m. from Custer Peak Lookout Tower, the photograph above shows the buildup of smoke from the McVey fire. Smoke is drifting east, but the burn is running almost due north. The McVey fire is considered one of the worst fires in Black Hills' history. A lightening strike or an out-of-control campfire was thought to be the cause of the four-day fire north of Hill City. The blaze started on July 8, 1939, and consumed 12 million board feet of saw timber, 18,000 acres of young trees, 17 cabins, and 100 head of cattle. The image below is of Job Corps workers using the Osborne Fire Finder on Custer Peak on August 10, 1967.

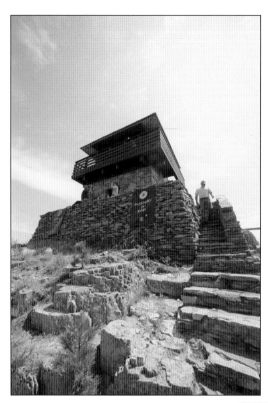

The Passport in Time program (PIT) is a volunteer archaeology and historic preservation program sponsored by the USDA Forest Service. Supervised by professionals, volunteers work on archaeological projects, restorations, research, oral history, and other preservation activities. In 2008, volunteers of Passport in Time worked with the Black Hills National Forest to repair portions of Custer Peak Tower, which was built in 1941 by the Civilian Conservation Corps. Weather and aging had caused the tower to deteriorate.

Veterans Peak Lookout, at an elevation of 5,338 feet, is located five miles south-southwest of Sturgis. Pictured is the original log tower under construction in 1939.

Veterans Peak Lookout is pictured in 1939. Unfortunately the uniquely designed log tower, built by the CCC, is no longer standing. The tower had been removed sometime in the 1950s. Apparently a tower was no longer needed, and it was not replaced. A radio tower now occupies the lookout site.

Pictured is the summit of Terry Peak on June 12, 1936, looking toward Custer Peak. Because of the elevation and it being the third-highest point east of the Rocky Mountains, as well as its vertical drop of 1,100 feet, Terry Peak would not only become a lookout site but would also become a popular skiing destination in the Midwest. (C.C. Averill.)

TERRY PEAK LOOKOUT

Terry Peak Lookout occupies an elevation of over 7,000 feet and is located four miles southwest of Lead. The lookout was named in honor of Gen. Alfred Terry and was in use until the late 1970s.

The Terry Peak Lookout Tower dates back to 1949, when a stone base and a small tower structure were initially built. In the 1960s, a larger living-quarter section was added in between the stone and tower structure. Water leakage and other safety concerns created maintenance problems. By 1973, the fire lookout tower was no longer used for its original purpose. The tower was closed for a time until a safety evaluation could be assessed. The Forest Service decided to remodel the structure, and the top lookout post and the middle section were removed and replaced with an open viewing deck at a cost of $16,700. Used as a visitor center, the lookout continues to draw a great number of people after it was remodeled.

The Bald Mountain Ski Club installed a rope tow in 1936. The first ski lift was in use in 1952; the longest run on Terry Peak is .8 miles. There are 450 acres of skiable terrain, 225 acres can be covered by a snowmaker, and 30 ski trails are available for use.

Vernon Tollefson is seen with the Osborne Fire Finder on Terry Peak. Tollefson and his wife, Diana, were lookouts at Cement Ridge and spent their honeymoon there. In the 1950s, they were transferred to Terry Peak. When at Terry Peak, Diana rode to the creek for their water and to the mining town of Tinton for their mail.

The site for the Seth Bullock Lookout was selected on June 9, 1942. The original tower was made of logs and wood. In the early 1900s, Pres. Theodore Roosevelt named the mountain Seth Bullock to honor his friend's service as a US marshal in South Dakota and as the second supervisor of the Black Hills National Forest from 1901 to 1906. Roosevelt described Seth Bullock as an "ideal American." Seth Bullock had been a miner, prospector, cattleman, and sheriff by the turn of the century before he became a forest supervisor. He took his job as supervisor seriously and delivered a message three years later that included these words, "The object of the forest reserve," he said, "is for the purpose of preserving the living and growing timber, promoting the younger growth and the regulation of the water supply. The dependence of the latter for a sure and sustained flow is wholly upon vegetation, which prevents rapid run off, and is best attained by a dense and vigorous growth of timber."

At an elevation of 5,971 feet, the Seth Bullock Lookout Tower, pictured here in 1943, is located 14 miles west-southwest of Rapid City. Seth Bullock, the lookout's namesake, also stated, "The permanent industries of the Black Hills are wholly dependent upon timber and water: destroy one, and these industries will disappear; while, if both are destroyed, the 'richest 100 miles square' will become a desert."

This wooden tower was removed in 1975. In this image, the old Seth Bullock Tower is coming down. The caption that is paired with the image reads, "They had a blast that day."

The old Seth Bullock Tower is now history in this image as it comes down; the wooden tower was removed in 1975. The log tower is gone, but the old stone steps and stairs are still there.

Seth Bullock Lookout Tower overlooks Pactola Dam. From the visitor center, one can drive to the south end of Lake Pactola to Custer Gulch Road and then on to County Road 25 to the 53-foot, all-steel, live-in tower. The man-made Lake Pactola flooded the old mining town of Pactola.

The Seth Bullock Mountain is also known as Scruton Mountain. The tower is easy to see from different vantage points in the area. The steel tower sits about 100 feet from the previous one.

Flag Mountain, with an elevation of 6,921 feet, is located 35 miles west of Rapid City in the Deerfield vicinity. CCC recruit Claire Patterson shared his experiences working on the construction of the Flag Mountain Lookout Tower. In 1941, the CCC was asked to build a tower at the top of Flag Mountain. The lower base of the lookout was built of local stone and cut on site. The upper portion was made of wood. According to Patterson, the CCC workers were required to haul the building materials up the side of the mountain to a point that was 200 to 300 feet from the building site. From here on, the terrain was very steep.

To overcome this obstacle, CCC recruits placed the cut stone in a bucket, which could hold up to 100 pounds. The bucket was attached to a cable that ran from the work area to the construction site. A pulley, attached to a tree at the lower end and to the framework of the tower above, operated when two harnessed men were attached to the main cable. They walked downhill, creating tension that pulled the loaded bucket to the top. The stone was taken out, and a flagman signaled the men to walk back up the hill, which allowed the empty bucket to go back down the slope for another load. This process was repeated many times a day and worked well for the sand and mortar mix also.

All that remains of the original lookout is a sample of the CCC recruits' hard work—the stone workmanship. The stones were cut to the required size below the tower site and then hauled to the top in buckets. The privy still exists, but the roof has deteriorated.

The Flag Mountain Lookout Tower, which was once perched on the edge of a rock outcropping, commanded views of Harney Peak and Reynolds Prairie, or Pe Sla, which means "bald place." Reynolds Prairie is considered by the Lakota to be a sacred site, a place to prepare for spring and to offer prayers of peace and healing. The sweep of the prairie, rimmed by forested hills, provides grazing for cattle and wildlife and vistas of peace and solitude to those who happen to discover its beauty.

Although not a fire lookout tower, the Roosevelt Tower is significant to the Black Hills history. Over the years, the tower has suffered from deterioration. In 2004, the Job Corps placed a mortar cap on the tower's base. However, the tower has been steadily deteriorating, causing the stairs to the observation deck to be closed. In 2009, stimulus money was awarded to national forest projects. Some of the funding will be used for stabilizing the tower.

General Wood & Capt. Bullock
at Roosevelt Monument
Dedication Day July 4 1919

Gen. Leonard A. Wood and former national forest supervisor Seth Bullock are photographed at the dedication of the Roosevelt Tower Monument on July 4, 1919. After Bullock heard of his friend Teddy Roosevelt's death in January 1919, he, with the help of the Society of Black Hills Pioneers, built the tower in Roosevelt's memory. Bullock, who was also Deadwood's first sheriff, saw the tower, also called the "Friendship Tower," finished shortly before his own death in September 1919. General Wood developed a friendship with Theodore Roosevelt when Roosevelt was assistant secretary of the Navy. Both Wood and Roosevelt organized the first volunteer cavalry regiment known as the Rough Riders at the outbreak of the Spanish-American War. Wood is known for his many military accomplishments and controversies. (J.N. McDerrough.)

Four

SUMMIT RIDGE AND SOUTHERN BLACK HILLS FIRE LOOKOUT TOWERS

Ed Mason's CCC crew built the original tower on Summit Ridge in 1935, located a half mile from its present site near the Wyoming border east of Newcastle, Wyoming. Each side was framed on the ground, and then two of the sides were tipped up and held while the cross members were attached. Once the entire tower was assembled, it was tipped up into upright positions.

CCC enrollees assigned to Summit CCC Camp, located at the head of Boles Canyon, worked on a log lookout tower to be located near Moon, South Dakota. Note the corner timbers are attached to pitch stubs, which are set in the ground. The tower was built of native ponderosa pine cut a half mile from the site. The completed tower stood 40 feet high and was six feet by six feet in diameter. Once the tower was built, it was manned by two men from the CCC 24 hours a day. The lookouts were expected to help put out the fires they spotted.

The Forest Service realized that the tower had been built on private land in Wyoming when they brought in a telephone line. A crew of workers was acquired to move the lookout by balancing it on chains between two small Cletrac 35 tractors. This close-up view shows the tower's attachment to log skids, which helped it slide across the ground.

Workmen appear to be finishing up the construction of the Summit Ridge Tower. The tower was used on this spot for five years before it was moved again to another ridge south of Moon Campground and renamed the Moon Tower. The lookout was occasionally staffed for 20 years before it was sawed down and partially buried in 1960.

Listed on national Historic Lookout Register, this tower was built in 1939–1940 at an elevation of 6,096 feet. Summit Ridge has not been staffed on a regular basis since 1972 but is used periodically to pinpoint smoke after a dry lightning storm. Summit Ridge was one of the more impressive lookouts in the southern Black Hills, as it had two phone lines instead of the customary one. Summit Ridge served as a relay station between the supervisor's office in Custer and the other lookout towers.

When Elk Mountain received electricity, Summit Ridge was downgraded as a secondary lookout. The steel tower on Summit Ridge was first used in 1940 and was staffed by Jesse Scott, a local rancher. Summit Ridge is identical to Elk Mountain's steel tower. They were built by Aermotor of Chicago.

Identical cabins at Elk Mountain and Summit Ridge were built at the same time to provide living quarters for the lookouts. Logs were cut on the respective sites and then taken to Custer for fitting, where they became mixed up. Summit received the Elk Mountain logs and vice versa, but the mix-up was discovered too late. The cabin measures 22 feet by 32 feet and has three rooms and a single-car garage connected to the kitchen and bedroom.

Elk Mountain is located 20 miles west of Custer at an elevation 5,669 feet. The US Forest Service operates this lookout. The Aermotor Company of Chicago, especially known for its windmill construction, built the steel tower in 1940. The Aermotor towers cost from $400 to $800, and the cabs measured four feet by four feet to eight feet by eight feet. The Elk Mountain cab measures seven feet by seven feet; the tower itself is 67.5 feet tall. The tower was built according to a standard plan, the same plan used for its sister tower, Summit Ridge. These utilitarian structures are not known for their architecture esthetics like the towers built by the CCC workers in the 1930s, when more emphasis was placed on the towers blending in with their surroundings. Ed Hawley, a local rancher, worked at Elk Mountain during this time.

The entrance to the one-room tower cab is located in the floor and swings down. After the door is closed, it becomes part of the cab floor again. The inside of the cab is paneled with plywood. The hinged map board folds up against the ceiling. The cab is strictly utilitarian and is supplied with the necessary equipment. Although the lookout is not intended to be a live-in cab, Minnie Cooper, who manned the tower for 15 years, had a cot cut down to size so she could spend nights in the tower tracking lightning.

B. Ralph Marshall was the alternate lookout on three different towers, including Elk Mountain in 1962. That year, a wire safety net was installed on the zigzagging stairs along with electricity.

Since the tower is not a live-in model, a cabin was built in 1941 out of logs for the lookout employee. The rectangular structure, saddle-notched at the corners, contained a single-car garage that occupied one end of the building, with two rooms on the other end. The cabin was located to the east of the tower, and the privy was to the north. The cabin had been altered at a later date by converting the garage to living space and installing a shower in 1982. Unfortunately, the Elk Mountain fire of 2002 burned everything but the lone standing tower.

Bear Mountain is located west of Crazy Horse Memorial. The first lookout tower on Bear Mountain was constructed in 1913. Many of the first lookouts rode saddle horses to the mountain's summit, as there were not any roads. The cab has not yet been added in this image.

This image is dated June 14, 1913, and was taken by the Harney National Forest supervisor Richard P. Imes. Imes served from 1910 to 1916. During his tenure, he was involved with the restocking of the national forests with over 10 tons of tree seed sown nationwide. Seed cost 75 cents per pound according to a June 11, 1912, forest service report on reforestation. When the seed was received, it became apparent to the forest officer in charge that it was not of good quality. It was determined that 43 percent of the seed was composed of broken glass, pieces of wire nails, gravel, pieces of coal, seed scales, seed wings, pine needles, and other foreign substances.

Bear Mountain is so named because of the number of bears said to have roamed there in the early days. The original tower was modified with a large wooden cab in 1923. The legend of Bear Trap Cave may be proof of bears' existence in the area. A deep cave, naturally camouflaged, became a death trap for a bear that entered through a hole at the top. Once inside the deep cave, the bear found out he could not climb out, leaving deep claw marks on the walls. His bones and skull were found years later.

Two men identified as Bren and Slavak stand on the steps of the wooden tower at Bear Mountain Lookout. Gail Duncan was one of the dedicated lookouts who manned Bear Mountain. She worked for 45 years between the years 1946 and 1981. She, like other lookouts, enjoyed the "peaceful existence" experienced at the top of the world.

Located 12 miles northwest of Custer and west of the Crazy Horse Memorial, Bear Mountain, with an elevation of 7,166 feet, is considered to be in the center of the Black Hills. The 30-foot, all-steel, live-in tower is manned during the summer months. The current steel tower has an enclosed glass cab surrounding it, which replaced a wooden cab that was constructed at an earlier date. The US Forest Service is in charge of Bear Mountain.

The communications log from Bear Mountain in 1983 is an interesting record of the days spent there by several different lookouts. Each day, the log opens with a comment regarding weather conditions. A cool, wet day usually meant a day with little action, which was summed up with a comment such as "a long, cool day." But other times, certain comments and reports almost guaranteed a busy, exciting day: heavy lightning, a hot day, a wicked storm coming in, high wind, heat lightning, and the ultimate remark, smoke visible. The phone was out on occasion that year, probably causing some anxious moments.

Castle Peak is located 25 miles west of Rapid City at an elevation of 6,362 feet. The CCC built a wooden fire lookout sometime between 1936 and 1939. A cabin and a garage were also built to provide living quarters for the lookout personnel. (Courtesy June Johnston.)

In 1964, a fire burned the site. By this time, most of the lookout towers had outlived their usefulness. Not much remains except the cement pylons and a bronze disc geological survey marker. The tower was a wooden superstructure, as evidenced by the metal straps extending up from the cement pylons. If it had been a metal structure, bolts would have been implanted in the cement instead.

Norris Peak is located in the Pactola Dam Quadrangle, USGS, eight miles west of Rapid City, at an elevation of 4,982 feet. Many lookout towers began as a platform placed in a tree. Spikes were driven in the trunk so the lookout could climb to the top. In the image below, the platform can be seen amid the surrounding trees. Eventually a six-foot-diameter lookout nest atop a 60-foot tower replaced the platform in the trees. The new tower was built in 1938 by the CCC. The closest water source was reported to have been Wild Irishman Gulch, and the dominant vegetation was ponderosa pine, blue stem, and poison ivy.

The CCC workers built Norris Peak Tower in 1938. The 60-foot tower supported a six-foot-diameter lookout nest. When the tower was no longer needed, it was put out of service and demolished in 1966. Norris Peak was not a live-in tower, so a cabin was built alongside for the lookout personnel and their families. A pit was dug and used for food storage. (June Johnston.)

When archaeologists visited the site long after it was demolished, they located five features, including tower pilings, shed foundation, two pits, and a fire ring. Rocks that once covered the area were organized into a driveway boundary.

The Crow's Nest Tower, once located 40 miles west of Rapid City and about 8 miles northwest of Deerfield, is no longer there. At one time, the site had a 70-foot-high steel tower with a screened cab. It was selected as a site for a tower on June 9, 1942. The tower that once occupied a 7,491-foot elevation has been removed.

Boulder Hill Lookout, which has an elevation of 5,335 feet, is located six miles northeast of Mount Rushmore and two miles northwest of Rockerville. Typical of the many steel fire towers throughout the Black Hills, Boulder Hill's usefulness came to an end. Concrete blocks and steps are all that remain, and unfortunately very little information has survived.

Five

MOUNT COOLIDGE AND CENTRAL BLACK HILLS FIRE LOOKOUT TOWERS

Mount Coolidge is located in Custer State Park, 10 miles south of Mount Rushmore, at an elevation of 6,023 feet. From dispatching personnel to fight fires to relaying location of buffalo herds, it is the hub of the park's communication system. Radio messages can be sent to all fire trucks and men in the area. The State of South Dakota maintains this lookout.

PRESIDENT COOLIDGE
WEIGHING HIS FIRST
CATCH.

(C-9) RISE
STUDIO

President Coolidge and First Lady Grace Coolidge spent the summer of 1927 at the State Game Lodge. In the photograph above, the president displays fish he caught in Grace Coolidge Creek. The car took him 32 miles each day to Rapid City High School where his offices were located. Mount Coolidge was formerly called Sheep Mountain because of the big horn sheep that occupied its slopes. In the summer of 1927, the mountain was renamed in honor of President Coolidge in memory of his visit to the state.

PRESIDENT and MRS. COOLIDGE ARE
PRESENTED with RAPID CANYON WILD FLOWERS.

RISE
PHOTO
C-29

In 1923, the US Forest Service built the first Mount Coolidge Lookout Tower on the highest peak in the southern section of the Black Hills. After the tower was built, the mountain was renamed Lookout Mountain. In this image, it appears that the tower has just been completed.

Images of the tower were used on postcards that tourists purchased and mailed back home. A summary on one card reads, "Mount Coolidge, formerly called Sheep Mountain, was renamed after the visit of Pres. Calvin Coolidge to the Black Hills in 1927. A good auto road leads to the top of the mountain, altitude 6,400 feet, from where a vista unequaled in beauty is obtainable. From a fire lookout tower, 75 feet high, the vigilance of forest rangers guards against devastating fires and protect mountain timber."

In 1938, the road to Mount Coolidge was considered the most thrilling in the Black Hills. The fire tower on Mount Coolidge became a tourist destination. Steep slopes dropped away on either side with no guardrails. The log tower had an inside staircase, from which three states could be viewed: South Dakota, Nebraska, and Wyoming. The immense tower dwarfs the woman standing on the steps in this image.

The CCC built the new Mount Coolidge stone lookout tower in 1940. Men of Camp Narrows, located near Blue Bell Lodge, replaced the wooden tower with a rock and stone lookout. From the tower, one can view Crazy Horse Mountain, Mount Rushmore, the Needles, Ellsworth Air Force Base, and the Badlands on a clear day. The turnoff to the tower is located on South Dakota Highway 87. A 1.7-mile gravel road takes one on a thrilling ride to the mountain's summit. From there, Crazy Horse Monument, Harney Peak, and Mount Rushmore can be viewed. (Above, Jan Cerney; at right, Roberta Sago.)

Cicero Peak Lookout, at an elevation of 6,166 feet, was located six miles south-southeast of Custer. The members of the CCC Camp Mayo built the lookout tower in 1939. Tower service was discontinued in 1973. There is a Forest Service communication tower at the top and a road that one can take all the way to the summit.

June Johnston went to work at Cicero in the summer of 1964 and was the last lookout on the peak, ending her duties in 1972. She took both her sons with her when they were just babies. She said her younger son "went to the tower with us when he was five months old. He used to crawl around on the catwalk and back down the first flight of stairs, where he would sit on the catwalk to catch the breeze. When he got tired, he would crawl back up the stairs and into the tower." Lookout duty was a "family job," she also added.

The lookout tower on Cicero Peak was removed from the peak and driven unceremoniously down the main street of Custer on a truck on March 19, 1980.

Built in 1939–1940, Cicero's tower was used for 34 years and then taken out of service in 1974. The tower was declared surplus and sold to a Custer man, who in turn sold it to Marine Life in Custer to use as a tourist tower.

Located one mile northeast of Hot Springs, the Battle Mountain Lookout Tower is used only during extreme conditions and is maintained by the State of South Dakota. Battle Mountain Lookout Tower, at an elevation of 4,434 feet, is a short tower with no cab. Battle Mountain was so named as it was the site of a battle between the Sioux and the Cheyenne for the possession of the warm and healing springs below the mountain. The Cheyenne had been in possession of the springs until the Sioux waged war.

Rankin Ridge is located in Wind Cave National Park, 10 miles southeast of Custer at an elevation of 5,013 feet, making it the highest point in the park. It was named after William A. Rankin, the first superintendent of the park, who began his service in August 11, 1903. Rankin Ridge is at the southern boundary of the Black Hills. Since the tower is located in a national park, the US Department of Interior operates this lookout.

A 72-stair climb leads to the top of the tower, which is rarely staffed except during times of extreme fire danger. A steel fire tower replaced a wooden tower built in 1952. As an extra bonus to visitors of Rankin Ridge, 14 interpretive stops are placed along the one-mile-loop nature trail that takes one through a ponderosa pine forest. (Wind Cave National Park.)

Inside, cozy living quarters provided a place to cook, eat, and sleep while the lookout was on duty. The refrigerator and stove used propane, and water was delivered by a gravity-fed water supply on the roof. Since there was no electricity, a lantern provided light. The one drawback to this pleasant scene at the top of the world was the lack of indoor plumbing. (Wind Cave National Forest.)

Lynn Frary uses binoculars to look for signs of smoke. When lookouts knew the terrain well, they were invaluable to determining the location of a possible fire. (Wind Cave National Park.)

In this image, the Osborne Fire Finder, binoculars, a map, and a knowledgeable lookout are clearly seen; all were necessary for fire suppression. Most of the fire lookouts either grew up in the country that they were working in or had walked it to become familiar with its every ravine and hill. To know the lay of the land was a necessary advantage in spotting fires. (Wind Cave National Park.)

Pilger Peak is located in Custer County at an elevation of 4,793 feet. Both Parker Peak and Pilger Peak Lookout Towers oversaw the southern Black Hills. Neither of the towers is standing today. Signal Hill was another southern Black Hills lookout, located 12 miles west-northwest of Custer at an elevation of 6,483 feet. Signal Hill's tower was also removed. (June Johnston.)

Parker Peak is located between Hot Springs and Edgemont. The 30-foot wooden tower was built at Parker Peak in 1941. The plans were initiated in 1940 for both Parker Peak and Pisgah Mountain. A garage and latrine were requested in 1944 for both. Gail and Herbert Duncan spent 20 years at Parker Peak as lookouts. (June Johnston.)

Parker Peak had maintenance problems that were typical of all the fire towers. In 1947, the guy wires at the peak had sagged, and the tower swayed considerably in strong winds. It was recommended that the guys be tightened. In 1953, the stairway was deemed unsafe. It was steep, and the overlapping treads made it dangerous when walking down the stairs unless coming down backwards. When the treads were wet or covered with ice or snow, the danger increased. A recommendation was made that the stairs be redone. The tower is no longer standing. (June Johnston.)

Six

BLACK HILLS FIRE LOOKOUT TOWERS IN BEAR LODGE MOUNTAIN

Pres. Theodore Roosevelt's presidential proclamation of 1907 created the Bear Lodge National Forest, with headquarters in Sundance. The Sundance National Forest merged with the Black Hills National Forest in 1915.

Warren Peak, at an elevation 6,434 feet, is located eight miles north of Sundance, Wyoming, in the Bear Lodge Mountains. The Black Hills National Forest extends into Wyoming. The approximately 170,000 acres of Wyoming's northeast corner is known as the Bear Lodge Mountains.

Warren Peak was the site for military radar used for surveillance of aircraft entering US air space in the 1960s and 1970s. Nearby Sundance was one of 143 radar installations in the northern portion of the United States during the Cold War era. Sundance became home to the Sundance Air Force Station on April 19, 1961. The United States' first nuclear-powered radar was located here.

To provide power for the radar station, the first "portable medium range power plant," which was a nuclear power plant, was installed in October 1961. The Martin Company built the plant for the Atomic Energy Commission. For the next seven years, PM-1 was the location for a series of experiments to prove that this kind of operation was a viable source of power. When the experiments were completed, PM-1 closed in April 1968. Beyond the power plant, one can see the steel lookout Warren Peak Tower on the horizon.

The original lookout structure was built by the CCC in 1938 and was a half mile west of the present-day steel tower. The original tower was used for 22 years and had a phone line for reporting fires. Radio communication became available in 1945. Maurice Classick, who staffed Warren Peak for 30 years, was not only with the crew that built the wooden tower but also helped tear it down. Classick was also involved with the construction of the steel tower that replaced it. Classick witnessed some of the worst lightning on May 7, 1944, while he worked the peak. He was in the old 10-foot tower when "the lightning struck an overhead roof antenna, burned up our radio and telephone, and burned holes in the bed. The bolt stopped three feet short of my head," said Classick in an interview. Dixie Boyle acted as a lookout in the Black Hills for a number of years and has never experienced lighting at its worst at Warren Peak. She says that the "lightning rods start humming before the lightning is ready to strike."

This lookout was photographed on September 26, 1944. Since the lookout staff spent many hours here in isolation, conveniences were provided. A table and chairs and a stove are pictured. Notice the forest fire danger meter on the backside of the table. (Jay Higgins.)

A bed and cabinets are seen in these two photographs. The fire lookout towers were a home away from home. In the early days, lookouts were required to rustle up their own food, water, and wood. Everything was cooked on a wood stove, as there was no electricity provided. It took a special person not only to handle the loneliness, but to be able to spring into action when smoke was spotted. (Jay Higgins.)

One of the landmarks visible from the top of the Warren Peak Tower is Devil's Tower. This remarkable formation is a column of igneous rock that rises 1,267 feet out of the surrounding grasslands. The formation is also called Mato Tipila, or "bear lodge," by the Lakota and is sacred to many Native American peoples. Several legends surround the tower. One of these is that there were several young girls playing on the rocks, when a bear came along to eat them. They climbed to the highest rock but were not out of the bear's reach. Then the Great Spirit intervened, causing the ground to grow, taking the girls out of the bear's reach. As the bear reached for the girls, he scratched the sides of the rock and caused the vertical marks on the side of the formation. The tower became popular among locals as a spot for picnicking and camping and was in danger of exploitation by private individuals. In 1892, Wyoming senator Francis E. Warren applied to the General Land Office to protect the tower and nearby Little Missouri River Buttes. Under the provision of the Forest Reserve Act of 1891, the General Land Office set aside 60.5 square miles in this area as a forest reserve. To insure long-term protections of the area, a movement to make the tower and buttes a national park developed. Following the Antiquities Act of June 1906, Frank W. Mondell Newcastle, Wyoming resident and Wyoming representative at large, joined the campaign to make Devil's Tower a national monument. On September 24, 1906, Pres. Theodore Roosevelt proclaimed Devil's Tower as the first national monument. The buttes were not included and were later opened to settlement. (W.R. Cross Collection, Case Library.)

The Basalt Peak, known as Inyan Kara, is a molten intrusion that never erupted. Over a period of millions of years, this laccolith has uplifted and eroded to stand 1,200 feet above the prairie. Inyan Kara is the most prominent peak on the west side of the Black Hills. As they traveled across the plains to the Black Hills, early expeditions watched it for miles. Its mysterious grandeur drew Lieutenant Warren and his expedition in 1857, Gen. George Custer and his expedition in 1874, and the Newton-Jenny expedition in 1875 to explore its surface. Archaeologists have discovered quarries and hearths upon the mountain, indicating early Indian use. C.C. Averill photographed the image above on August 25, 1938.

Located in Wyoming near Newcastle, this new Mount Pisgah Fire Lookout Tower is being constructed beside the old log fire tower at Mount Pisgah in 1957. The old 45-foot fire tower was built at the same time as Parker Peak Lookout in 1941. Telephone and lightning protection systems were installed at both the original towers of Pisgah and Parker. (R. Osborn.)

The photograph on the right shows the original Cement Ridge Lookout Tower. By September 6, 1938, the date on the image below, the cabin had been removed. The photographer listed this photograph is Clarence C. Averill, who served as supervisor from 1939 to 1941 and 1948 to 1954. (Crook County Museum.)

Cement Ridge, located in Wyoming just across the South Dakota border, has been used as a lookout site since 1912. This current lookout is the third structure to occupy Cement Ridge. In the beginning, a log cabin was used as a lookout and living quarters until a wooden tower was constructed near the cabin in 1921. A 14-by-14-foot cabin built on a 10-foot-tall tower replaced the first log cabin. With great difficulty, Tom Sawyer, his wife, and son brought the first vehicle to the top of Cement Ridge in 1927. He placed a sack of potatoes behind the rear wheels to prevent the vehicle from rolling downhill as he cleared brush in front in order to proceed. Since there was not a road to the summit, he remained there with his family for the rest of the summer, while the Forest Service used a mule train to pack in their supplies.

These photographs show the interiors of the Cement Ridge's towers. They illustrate the "conveniences and equipment in primary lookout towers." In the image above, one sees a lookout using communication equipment; the date is September 6, 1938. In the photograph at right, one sees the Fire Finder Alidade and forest map; the date is September 26, 1944. (Jay Higgins photographer; Crook County Museum.)

The Civilian Conservation Corps built a stone tower in 1941, one of the last CCC projects. A 14-by-14-foot cabin topped a 10-foot tower. Cement Ridge had no electricity and used solar panels to power the radio. In 1993, the Cement Ridge Lookout was listed on the National Historic Register. In 2006, the tower was restored and manned full-time. (Del Harding.)

Panoramic views of western Wyoming, as well as Crow Peak, Terry Peak, and Custer Peak in South Dakota, can be seen from the Cement Ridge Lookout Tower. Interpretive exhibits are displayed in the lower level. The building is open for snowmobilers and skiers to warm themselves during the winter; however, vandals have taken advantage of Cement Ridge's open-door policy. (Roberta Sago.)

In addition to the sweeping vistas, there are many things to see more close at hand. Spring visitors to Cement Ridge may be treated to the site of the pasqueflower. Typically an early bloomer, this plant is named for the Easter season because it usually starts blooming in March and April. Its color ranges from white to deep lavender. The American pasqueflower can be found all across the High Plains. Thus, in 1903, it was named the state flower of South Dakota. In fact, it was the first designated South Dakota symbol. (Roberta Sago.)

The Lead, South Dakota, Homestake Mine used a pine tree for a fire lookout near Moskee, Wyoming, around 1924. A ladder placed at the bottom of the tall pine tree reached the spikes that were driven into the trunk of the tree for climbing. A more permanent structure, with a steel platform, was built after the 1936 Moskee fire.

Seven

SMOKEY BEAR AND FIRE PREVENTION

Smokey Bear, the US Forest Service mascot, is an American icon. He was created in 1944 by illustrator Albert Staehle. Smokey's original image showed him pouring a bucket of water on a campfire with the caption, "Smokey says—Caution will prevent 9 out of 10 forest fires." Smokey was preceded by several other fire-prevention campaigns. To reduce the losses from human-caused fires, President Roosevelt introduced an ad campaign in 1937. Uncle Sam as a forest ranger conveyed the message, "Your Forests—Your fault—Your Loss." Public awareness about the dangers of forest fires was increased in 1942. A Japanese submarine surfaced off the coast of California and fired on an oil field, endangering the Los Padres National Forest. Most of the experienced firefighters were involved in war endeavors. The Forest Service developed a public-service campaign with slogans such as "Do not aid the enemy" and "Our carelessness, their secret weapon." Enemy shelling did not long remain a danger to the forests.

Human carelessness causes thousands of wildfires every year. The most enduring slogan, "Remember—Only you can prevent forest fires," was developed in 1947. The message was updated in 2001 and became, "Only you can prevent wildfires," to include the dangers of fire in grasslands. Smokey Bear is one of the most successful and enduring public-service advertising campaigns.

According to Ellen Bidell in her article, "Happy 65th Birthday, Smokey Bear," most accidental fires are started by children. So the selection of a furry woodland creature to deliver the message of fire safety was a deliberate choice to appeal to youngsters. Smokey makes public appearances, where he meets children and shares his message.

This song, written in 1952, has caused some confusion about Smokey's proper name; it is Smokey Bear. However, in order to fit the music, the songwriters add the middle name of "the," but to refer to Smokey the Bear is incorrect. Smokey's image is administered by the US Forest Service, the National Association of Foresters, and the Ad Council and is protected by the Smokey Bear Act of 1952. Since that time, products bearing his image must be licensed. The conservation pledge was published on the back of the sheet music shown.

Like Smokey's slogan, his mission has evolved to reflect these times. He now must explain the difference between good fires and bad fires and how some fires play an important role in maintaining balance in the forest ecology. He now promotes responsible stewardship of natural resources.

Thus concludes this "armchair" tour of the Black Hills National Forest Fire Lookout Towers through time.

BIBLIOGRAPHY

Archaeology Center. Custer, SD.

Bearlodge Ranger District Office. Sundance, WY.

Bidell, Ellen. "Happy 65th Birthday Smokey Bear." *New York State Conservationist.* October 2009.

Black Hills National Forest Files. Headquarters: Custer, SD.

Black Hills National Forest Historical Collection: Black Hills State University, Leland D. Case Library. Spearfish, SD.

Boyle, Dixie. *Between Land and Sky.* Denver: Outskirts Press, 2007.

Congressional Record. Senate, September 18, 1979.

Fechner, Robert. "The Civilian Conservation Corps." *The Black Hills Engineer.* December 1937.

Federal Writers' Project. *A South Dakota Guide.* Pierre, SD: South Dakota State Historical Press, 1993.

Hickel, M.R. *Hickel Journal.* Spearfish, SD.

Higbee, Paul. "Packing Up Harney Peak." *South Dakota Magazine.* July/August 1996.

Larson, George, ed. "A CCC Recruit Looks Back: Claire Patterson's Black Hills Experience." *South Dakota Magazine.* Winter 2005, 35.4.

Mahoney, Mitch. *Centennial: Mini-Histories of the Black Hills National Forest.* Washington, DC: US Department of Agriculture, Forest Service: 1998.

Neihardt, John G. *Black Elk Speaks.* Lincoln, NE: University of Nebraska Press, 1961.

Remington, Nancy L. "Where There is Smoke, There is Fire!" *Black Hills Towers.*

Sanders, Peggy. *Wind Cave National Park.* Charleston, SC: Arcadia Publishing, 2003.

South Dakota State Historical Society.

www.radomes.org

www.arcadiapublishing.com

Discover books about the town where you grew up, the cities where your friends and families live, the town where your parents met, or even that retirement spot you've been dreaming about. Our Web site provides history lovers with exclusive deals, advanced notification about new titles, e-mail alerts of author events, and much more.

MADE IN THE USA

Arcadia Publishing, the leading local history publisher in the United States, is committed to making history accessible and meaningful through publishing books that celebrate and preserve the heritage of America's people and places. Consistent with our mission to preserve history on a local level, this book was printed in South Carolina on American-made paper and manufactured entirely in the United States.

This book carries the accredited Forest Stewardship Council (FSC) label and is printed on 100 percent FSC-certified paper. Products carrying the FSC label are independently certified to assure consumers that they come from forests that are managed to meet the social, economic, and ecological needs of present and future generations.

FSC
Mixed Sources
Product group from well-managed forests and other controlled sources

Cert no. SW-COC-001530
www.fsc.org
© 1996 Forest Stewardship Council

Find Your Place in History.